Blippy the Robot

by

Sonica Ellis

Illustrated by Nejla Shojaie

Copyright 2020
All Rights Reserved
ISBN: 978-0-578-69717-8

DEDICATION

This book is dedicated
to all my robot loving friends!

This book belongs to

_____

From:

_____

Blippy is a robot who is shiny and smart

with a computer for a brain and a clock for a heart.

His legs are short but his arms are long and his all-time hero is Captain Neil Armstrong.

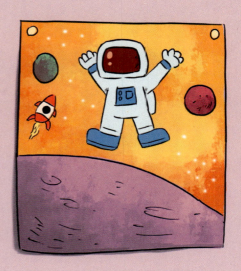

His eyes
   are like
       flashlights on the side of his head,
           and rather than feet
               are roller-skates instead!

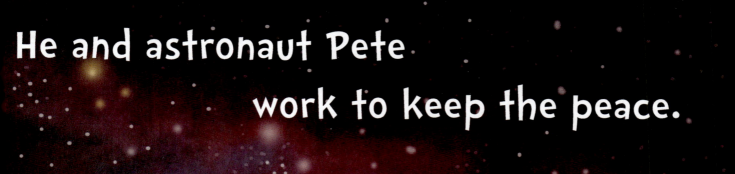

He and astronaut Pete work to keep the peace.

between Jupiter

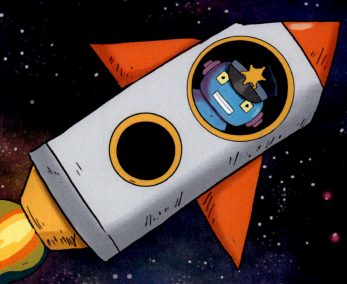

and

Mars...

So if you should

travel

along the Milky Way,

...and wish him "Good day!"

Blippy's Favorite Space Jokes!

Q: Why do robots take vacations?
A: To recharge their batteries!

Q: What is fast, loud and crunchy?
A: A rocket chip!

Q: What do robots wear in the winter?
   A: Roboots!

Q: How do you organize a space party?
   A: You planet!

Q: Why did Mickey Mouse go to space?
   A: To Find Pluto!

Q: What do robots do at lunch?
   A: Eat Megabytes!

It takes the Earth 365 days to travel around the sun!

If you could drive to the sun it would take 177 years!

Made in the USA
Monee, IL
20 July 2020